SWEET WISDOM
—— FOR ——
LIFE'S JOURNEY

SEEING THROUGH THE EYES OF YOUR HEART

Yvonne D. Coates, Ph.D.

Largo, MD

Copyright © 2022 Yvonne D. Coates, Ph.D.

All rights reserved under the international copyright law. No part of this book may be reproduced or transmitted in any form or by any means, electronic or mechanical, including photocopying, recording, or by any information storage and retrieval system, without the express, written permission of the publisher or the author. The exception is reviewers, who may quote brief passages in a review.

Christian Living Books, Inc.
christianlivingbooks.com
We bring your dreams to fruition.

ISBN 9781562295653

Unless otherwise noted, Scripture quotations are taken from the New International Version®, Copyright © 1973, 1978, 1984, 2011 by Biblica, Inc.® Used by permission of Zondervan. Scripture quotations marked (ESV) are taken from the English Standard Version®, Copyright © 2001 by Crossway, a publishing ministry of Good News Publishers. Scripture quotations marked (TLB) are taken from The Living Bible copyright © 1971. Used by permission of Tyndale House Publishers. All rights reserved.

Contents

Dedication v

Introduction vii

Chapter 1. The Journey Begins 1

Chapter 2. Stepping into My Purpose 5

Chapter 3. A Look Within 17

Chapter 4. Family Does Matter:
                Rooted in Faith and Inspiration 27

Chapter 5. Finding My Way 45

Chapter 6. Expectations and Experiences 59

Chapter 7. Growth Through Connections 71

Chapter 8. Change Is Inevitable 79

Chapter 9. The Journey Continues 85

Bibliography 89

About the Author 93

Dedication

I DEDICATE THIS BOOK to my parents, Jesse and Ella Diggs, who are both deceased. I honor them for their endurance, love, compassion, and faith. They instilled in me the concept of hard work, respect for others, and reaching back to help someone else. To Cecil and Yvette, my siblings, who always encourage and support me unconditionally. To Kathy, my North Carolina "sister-cuz," with whom I share a special bond of love and inspiration. To LaJuan and Mary, who showed me the joy of cruising. To my neighbor, Ulysses, whose favorite saying is "You never know what you gonna do when you get up in the morning." To my Peace Baptist Church family for their continued spiritual guidance and motivation. And to my love, special friend, confidant, and travel partner, Dervin, thanks for allowing me to be me and for that gentle but persistent nudge of encouragement to get this done.

Introduction

> I pray that the eyes of your heart may be enlightened.
> (Ephesians 1:18a)

Seeing with Your Heart, Not with Your Eyes

What is the heart? The medical journals highlight the heart as a key component of our existence. While we understand the necessity of the physical aspects of this vital organ, we continuously relate the heart to our emotions and feelings. We constantly hear about our heartbreaks, heartthrobs, and hearts and souls. As a child, you would hear, "Cross your heart and hope to die" in acknowledging the truth. If we do what we believe is right, we follow our hearts. If we change our minds about something, we have a change of heart. And if we want an honest and open discussion with someone, we have a heart-to-heart talk. On Valentine's Day, the heart is the symbol of love.

> "Open the eyes of my heart... I want to see you."
> (Baloche, P., 1997. *Open the Eyes of My Heart, Lord.*)

What about the eyes? One would say they give us the ability to see. The eyes allow us to see the world around us. It is often said, "The eyes are the window to your soul." We make judgment calls about individuals based on what we see. We say, "I have my eyes on you!" But are we merely looking, instead of really seeing?

This book is not an autobiography. It is a book of reflections and collected writings about my experiences as I have continued to progress through life's journey. We often hear people say our journeys are a series of beginnings and endings. I choose to say they are more like constant adjustments to a new normal.

My goal in life was to become a teacher, and I dedicated myself to the field of education. During my undergraduate studies, I realized I also enjoyed writing. However, I chose to continue to pursue my first love—education. Now, in this senior stage of my life, I am writing my long-awaited book.

Traveling on life's highway exposes us to many different experiences, including love, loneliness, and uncertainty. Over the years, I have used writing as my release valve. At certain junctions, it was important for me to express my feelings through words and thoughts, not by having discussions with others. Now, I am sharing them with you.

I look back at my own bucket list—or what we now call the "living list"—filled with hopes, dreams, and aspirations. In retrospect, I realize following one's passion has no time constraints or restrictions. It only has compassion, love, and a willingness to move forward. It is what we feel in our hearts and not always what we see with our eyes that has the greatest impact on who we become.

A Thought

The world is a flower garden in which God is the gardener.
Plucking those flowers that have fulfilled their purpose,
And planting those flowers that are to bloom forth mankind.

(SPRING 1970, IMMACULATA COLLEGE OF WASHINGTON)

A Journey

It's a journey ... that I propose ... I am not the guide ... nor technical assistant ... I will be your fellow passenger...

Though the rail has been ridden ... winter clouds cover ... autumn's exuberant quilt ... we must provide our own guide-posts...

I have heard ... from previous visitors ... the road washes out sometimes ... and passengers are compelled ... to continue groping ... or turn back ... I am not afraid...

I am not afraid ... of rough spots ... or lonely times ... I don't fear ... the success of this endeavor ... I am Ra ... in a space ... not to be discovered ... but invented...

I promise you nothing ... I accept your promise ... of the same we are simply riding ... A wave ... that may carry ... Or crash...

It's a journey ... and I want ... to go...

NIKKI GIOVANNI

CHAPTER ONE

The Journey Begins

For most of my life, I have thought about my journey. It did not matter whether it was my career path or my personal decisions that set me on a path of discovery. I realize all we do in life is select a chosen highway, which can be filled with straightaways, curves, and unexpected bumps along the way. Sometimes, we have no roadmaps or GPS; we just venture out and go. Sometimes, we actually make a detailed plan that we believe will ensure success. We face our crossroads with anticipation and anxiety. Our journeys take different paths based on the expectations and experiences we encounter along the way.

I believe life is merely a journey through discovery that takes endurance and patience. Each day presents us with new opportunities to make a difference, not only in our lives but also in the lives of those who enter our circles. My own journey is founded on three basic principles: sacrifice, service, and life-long learning. Sacrifices are unavoidable in our desire to reach the goals we wish to achieve. I define service as an inherent need to help others without seeking materialistic gain as the promise for doing. And lastly, life-long learning embodies the realization that to do for others, it is also important to expand one's horizons through the following:

- Personal engagement with others
- Traveling to immerse oneself in various cultures
- Always seeking opportunities for continued growth

When I was in the 6th grade, I realized I wanted to be a teacher and travel to all the places in my geography book. I am so fortunate; I was able to follow both dreams. This ultimate desire to help others succeed and explore various cultures was passionate in my spirit. However, the financial burdens that came with going to college and traveling the world often had me pondering if this would indeed be my story. Teaching in various capacities for over 35 years and traveling to exotic places—Beijing, China (Great Wall), Europe, South America, Antarctica, the Middle East, and Singapore—are both dreams come true. I have recognized it is impossible to take this journey through life without the encouragement, dedication, and support of family, friends, and unsolicited strangers. And for that, I am truly grateful.

In life, one must have a vision, a plan of action, and the faith, belief, and stamina to carry it through. We must see people as extensions of our own beings and refrain from such critical and negative judgments without understanding the journeys that have led them to their places in life. Our eyes let us see but sometimes we are not seeing. It is our hearts that show empathy, compassion, and love. Let us continue to see with our hearts, not just with our eyes.

I recognize everyone must experience his own journey in life, and it is not to be compared with someone else's. However, I do believe as we progress through life, we must be cognizant that everyone takes a journey using his own pair of shoes. My journey has been filled with successes and failures, love and hurt, and an uncanny spirit of continued growth and stagnation. I have now reached a milestone where the moments of reflection and unforgettable memories are emotionally woven into my existence. However, be certain this is not the end of my journey because my shoes are laced up and I still walk!

CHAPTER TWO

Stepping into My Purpose

"My mission in life is not merely to survive, but to thrive, and to do so with some passion, some compassion, some humor, and some style." —Maya Angelou

"Honor your calling. Everybody has one. Trust your heart, and success will come to you." —Oprah Winfrey

I can remember growing up on Elliot Street and Kentucky Avenue and playing teacher with the neighborhood children. Whether it was making mud cakes, jumping rope, rocking the hula hoop, or sharing stories, I enjoyed it. In elementary school, I was fascinated by the lessons, especially reading and geography. Thinking back now, I realize what started as a passion folded into a purpose. How fortunate I was to have recognized early in life what I aspired to do. That was just step one! Over time, I watched this passion and purpose evolve into a precious gift.

Finding Your Passion

The adage states, "We learn by doing." The question is, "What are we doing?" We complain that our society has entered a realm of misplaced or non-existent values. Some believe too many of our young people have lost respect and exhibit an attitude of entitlement and self-worth. Our desires for materialistic competition have outweighed our compassion for helping others. One generation blames the other; yet, no one wants to take responsibility. We look for quick-fix solutions. Eldridge Cleaver, an activist, once stated, "You're either part of the solution or you're part of the problem." I chose to be part of the solution.

In life, it is important to find one's passion. So often, we look for others to make that determination for us or we follow a path that is really someone else's passion and will never be our own. My dad wanted me to be a nurse. However, having spent some of my childhood in the hospital with bouts of asthma, that was not an option for me. Teachers suggested various career paths. However, I knew in the 6th grade at Bryan Elementary School that I wanted to be a teacher. I began my career as an English teacher at Hart Junior High School and Friendship Educational Center, both located in the Anacostia area in Southeast D.C.

In December 1972, I entered my first classroom. What an interesting time! While I was able to benefit from the outcomes of the civil rights movement, I became aware of the societal inequalities that existed in some parts of the city. Unfortunately, to this day, some things have not changed. My class sizes ranged from thirty-five to forty students and the academic levels varied. For me, this began another lesson of service and sacrifice.

Although I was a native Washingtonian, I was not initially prepared for the cultural and economic complexities in my teaching community. Teaching provided me an opportunity to connect with a group of students and families—many in need of self-empowerment and encouragement. Regardless of any personal problems I had, they were dismissed daily when I entered those school walls. This educational journey helped to expand my own character and beliefs. I was reminded that people do the best they can under the circumstances they face. Who are we to be judgmental when we have not walked in their path of survival?

I learned to accept individuals in whatever stage they currently exist. What could I constructively offer? It is not always about materialistic gifts but more about seeing with your heart, not with your eyes. That journey and my forever passion have resulted in lifelong relationships with some students to this present day. Special thanks to Teresa, Paula, Paul, and Ornella—you know who you are.

Discover You!

In life, we must try to recognize our gifts to develop our passions. I am fulfilled when I am helping others achieve their dreams. Whether it is teaching English to middle school students, adults in a community school program, or incarcerated men in a nearby prison, this is my passion.

You must be passionate about what you do and believe in it. Take the time to figure out your gifts, regardless of those who may want to deter you. However, remember with gifts come abilities. All gifts must be fine-tuned.

Who Am I?

I am the caring spirit
In the midst of the storm
To lift the clouds
And to move you on.

I am the forceful wind
When you need that push
When you stray too far
And need to get back on track.

I am the smiling sunray that warms your heart
Breaking down that barrier
Of coldness and aloofness
Preventing you from growing.

I am the morning dewdrops
Trickling down your face
Releasing the pressures
That keep you bound.

I am the lovely flower
That loses its petals
Only to recreate new ones
For all to experience its beauty.

I am the many forces of nature
That keep one balanced.
I am the kindred soul
Doing for others.

I am who I am.

(KRAMER MIDDLE SCHOOL, SEPTEMBER 2004)

> "I cannot be a teacher without exposing who I am."
> —Paulo Freire

How Can You Teach If You Haven't Been Taught?

In April 2005, I was the keynote speaker at the Maryland Association of Teacher Educators' Teacher Candidates Awards Program. The event was held at Hood College in Frederick, Maryland. At that time, I was an assistant principal at Kramer Middle School. My topic, "How Can You Teach If You Haven't Been Taught?" focused on three important attributes of aspiring teachers: caring, competent, and committed. Reflecting now on that speech, I realize how pertinent this question was and how it remains a permanent part of my philosophy. What had I been taught? And what did I teach?

All through school, our family values focused on the need to learn all you could. While the neighborhood children eagerly visited the movie theaters on Saturdays, my brother and I spent Saturdays in the library. Not only were we required to read books, but we also had to write book reports and prepare oral presentations for our parents. Television was taboo! I can remember when classmates began to discuss a television show, I would enter the conversation as if I had seen it, while in truth, I had not viewed anything. However, the sacrifices were worth it. I developed an appreciation for reading and writing and decided to become an English teacher. When I look back at my 1968 Eastern Senior High School yearbook, the caption under my picture reads: "Archery Club, Honor Society, Future Teachers, and Booster's Club. Plans to be an English Teacher."

My parents taught me the importance of a good education. Each of my higher education experiences has broadened my own skills in the value of teaching and learning. I enjoyed the academic setting. I knew through research, I could begin to develop a repertoire of knowledge, competencies, and skills that would help me reach my goals. To teach, I had to be competent. My educational journey not only included university studies but also other professional development opportunities I readily seized. I had this ongoing thirst for learning.

My academic training prepared me to be a teacher, but my heart and soul taught me how to care. As I entered the doors of Hart Junior High School in 1972 with a feeling of enthusiasm and anxiety, I recall several students milling around the front lobby when they should have been in class.

I was hired to teach in one of the most troubling inner-city schools. The meeting with the principal was brief with one question that resonates in my head today: "Do you think you can control these students?" Control was not what I was seeking. I wanted to teach.

In this profession, you become an integral part of the lives of others. Whether it is your students, the parents, or the community, you realize the struggles and the challenges everyone faces. The adolescent years are filled with a roller coaster of emotions. The environment can be taunting, and some students come to you bearing the weight of the social inequities in their own lives. Many seek attention (whether positive or negative), and this personal engagement must be addressed before you can teach academics.

I cared about my students, and they cared about me. My standards for learning were high but I supported my students to the utmost so they could succeed. We worked during our breakfast meetings, lunch, and after school. It was important for my students to be successful in not just my class but also in all classes. Whatever it took, that is what I/we did. I look back at the student notes I received: "Thanks for being there when I really needed you." "A very good friend." "My best vice-principal," and "Remember to stay nice and stop wearing any shade of red." There is indeed a story behind the red suit I sometimes wore.

I remember when my homeroom class presented me with a plaque, "Dedicated Homeroom Teacher, Friendship

Educational Center 1985-1986." I treasure the cards and letters sent to me when my grandmother and dad died. The surprise farewell ceremony (retirement) with students and staff at Kramer Middle School and my family was filled with hugs and tears. I had been a "mother figure" to many of my students, thus, the name "Mama Coates." While my futile attempts to explain that it was time were ignored, I truly recognized the effect these relationships had on our lives. This was my passion, mission, and love.

A trip down memory lane can reveal one's character, strength, and commitment. From teaching English in several high poverty, underachieving secondary schools in the city to developing and implementing adult education programs for incarcerated youth and adults in an area prison system (Second Chance, D.C. Department of Corrections), I learned the delicacy of providing educational opportunities for those deemed lost while keeping myself mentally and physically afloat. I tried to be the best role model.

> "I still remember the day you left… I was sad and I cried because no one could replace my favorite teacher. I remember you gave us a cookout at your home. I must say any child that was blessed to have been taught by you is one lucky person. Thank you for being a milestone within my educational process." –Facebook post by former student Rochelle Reid (July 2014)

I miss my students and working in the schools. It was the ability to take students where they were and propel them into unforeseen territory that motivated me. It wasn't just about the teaching of English but also building the connections of human kindness. Additional photos of my students and me in various venues (school events, my office with the stuffed animals, school prom, About Face Program wearing my Thanksgiving apron at the family dinner) were pasted in the scrapbook. I wonder where they are now and if I really made a difference.

Teaching had always been my passion, which folded into my life mission and never-ending purpose. Growing up, I was taught the principles of the three Cs—caring, competent, and committed—that I have carried into my adulthood. As a teacher, one must have a caring and humble spirit. One must be prepared to do the job. Finally, one must be committed for the long haul. God gives each of us a gift to develop and use. My gift is one of service to others. That is why teaching and learning are so important to me. Knowledge is useless if it is not shared. I do for others, not for any selfish reason or motivation. I do it because I care. The question remains, "How can you teach if you haven't been taught?" The answer is—you can't.

(NOVEMBER 2021)

I Am a Teacher

I am a teacher. I awaken all minds.

I demonstrate **Tenacity** because my commitment is well-grounded.

I must teach by **Example** because I am indeed a role model.

My purpose is **Not Ambiguous**, for my destination is clear.

My **Caring** spirit is evident in my love for all children.

I exhibit a **High-Spirit** nature that will motivate myself and others.

My mission is **Empirica**l because learning must be reality-based.

I am **Responsible** for the sharing of knowledge and opening the doors of inquiry.

I am a professional—I am a teacher.

I awaken all minds.

(SEPTEMBER 1997)

> "I have a past that is rich in memories. I have a present that is challenging, adventurous, and fun because I spend my days with the future. I am a teacher and I thank God for it every day." –John Schlatter

CHAPTER THREE

A Look Within

"The only journey that matters is the journey within."
—Rainer Maria Rilke

While visiting my "sister-cuz" in North Carolina, I accompanied her to church one Sunday. The message given by Pastor Sneed was, "It's Not Over. It's Only Halftime." The emotional roller coaster of life can swing a person from high to low in a matter of seconds. Relationships are built then crumble and successes blossom then falter. In the search for peace and calm, it is important to take a moment to reflect. Each experience in life is a teachable moment. I discovered each day presents an opportunity to succeed. There is always hope, even in despair. When facing life's downward trend, remember it's not over; it's only halftime.

This Day Is Mine

The value of this day is impossible to measure
For it will never come again.
I do not wish to regret its passing.
What I do today is up to me and no one else.
I can use it to good advantage
Or squander it away.
The choice is mine.

I will try to make my day one of
Success rather than failure
Satisfaction rather than frustration
Joy rather than pain
Laughter rather than hate.

This day is mine.
I do not wish to regret its passing.

(100TH ANNIVERSARY, PEACE BAPTIST CHURCH, OCTOBER 2011)

Loneliness

Loneliness is a bitterness
That gnaws like a
Thousand termites
Until there is nothing—
But an empty shell.

Loneliness overtakes the body
Completely and wholly
Its vibe destroys all others
Drifting into a world without feelings
Without love
Without cares
Without you.

(APRIL 1976)

Giving Thanks

I sit and I wonder
Do they really know
The meaning of Thanksgiving
And all that it does bestow
The gladness of just being alive
And having food and shelter
The willingness to survive
In the world of unforeseen
Endeavors?

I sit and I wonder
Do they really care
For all those who do for them
And stand by when all is not fair.

The semblance of just knowing
That when the rough times do appear
There is someone to help guide them
And to really care?

I sit and I wonder
Have they really thought ahead
Prepared and asked themselves
Will I too ever be in need?
The need for just companionship

The need to just survive
The need to conquer mountains
The need to be alive.

And as I sit and wonder
What the day truly means
I thank God for His presence
And the satisfying of my needs.

And those times in which I grumble
May He truly understand
How quickly I have forgotten
All He has done for man.

(ENGLISH TEACHER, SECOND CHANCES PROGRAM,
DEPARTMENT OF CORRECTIONS, OCCOQUAN, 1985)

Springtime

Spring bursts forth with its rainbow of colors
Sheltering all in its path like a gigantic umbrella
Blocking the remnants of winter as it slowly withdraws
Until another time.

Hearts once subdued become alive
With new feelings
New emotions
New love.

It's spring!
Wrapping its beauty around our bodies
Revitalizing our souls with a new inner strength.

It's spring!

(APRIL 1987)

Holding On

With arms outstretched
Engulfing those feelings of tenderness
Which burst out like the pure darkness of night
With the twinkling of a seemingly intangible star
Seeking the infinite
Reaching
Searching.

I drift outward on the sea of calmness
To that special place of vision
Of song, of soul
Writing
Yearning.

For the concern heard from your voice
For the sincerity that emits from your eyes and
For the love of just caring from your heart.
With arms outstretched
Caring
Loving.

(APRIL 1987)

All Alone

My heart floats endlessly
Over the white tips of the ocean
Searching
And with each sensual dip of the wave
It aches
Because you are not with me.

I see you but you are not there
I feel you but you are not here
I want you but...

The beauty of love is like a thorn disguised
Inclusive of happiness and pain
That intertwines deeply within my soul
Not knowing which feeling will dominate
The inner struggle continues
Until ultimately the joy of your smile
And the sensitivity in your touch
Make the prickly pain of needing you
And wanting you not so unbearable!

I see you but you are not there
I feel you but you are not here
I want you but...

(NOVEMBER 1987)

CHAPTER FOUR

Family Does Matter: Rooted in Faith and Inspiration

"Honor your father and mother—which is the first commandment with a promise." (Ephesians 6:2)

"Teach a child to choose the right path, and when he is older, he will remain upon it." (Psalm 22:6 TLB)

Many say I am my "father's child"! On self-reflection, I do have many of my dad's characteristics. However, both of my parents have had a great influence on me. I do not think I really appreciated this as a child, but life's experiences always bring me back to their teachings. My parents taught me about high expectations, the value of learning, developing character, and having integrity. To my parents, my best friends, I say thanks!

"Dads share wisdom with their children in the hopes they spread it throughout the world." –Unknown

I'm Glad You're My Dad

I'm glad you're my dad
Because you make me feel so proud
Just knowing that you do care
With an encouraging compliment
Or a congratulatory smile.

I'm glad you're my dad
Because without you I wouldn't exist.
I would have never known
The glories of nature
Or feel the pleasure of your hug and kiss.

I'm glad you're my dad
Although your job was extremely hard
In getting me to understand
The rules of right and wrong.

As a young child
I didn't truly realize
All that you had to do
To enable us to survive.

But as I became an adult
And the complications of life
Knocked at my door
I remember those words of wisdom
As told by you before.

Now they function as my guiding light
As I try to progress on
I admired your strength and endurance
And have adopted them as my own.

And on this day of recognition
When all dads are to be praised
I wish the most to my loving father
Who is also my best friend.

(FATHER'S DAY, JUNE 1987)

I remember how I would write letters to my parents. It was a great way to surprise them and share my thoughts. We found this letter among my father's belongings after he passed. I can't remember the gift that accompanied the letter. However, just the fact that my dad kept this letter was meaningful to me. I recall one of my dad's favorite sayings: "I remember what I don't forget." I remember the trips to the Kalorama Skating rink (and I still have my skates!), the road trip to Florida and playing a game: "Name That State License Plate," the strict rules as only a parent can give, excitement about the money received when I brought home an "A" paper and a good report card from school, riding roller coasters, the purchase of my first car—a used Dodge Charger—the importance of saving money, and the frank discussions once I became an adult. Every time I reach back and revisit some of these special moments, it further acknowledges who I am today.

Dear Dad,

I just wanted to tell you just how special you are to me and how fortunate I am to have you as my dad. I think of all the fun times that we have had in the past and the ones that we will continue to have in the future. I love having you not only as my dad, but also as my friend. Sometimes it is not easy "being grown" and I am lucky to have two people in my life who will always be there for me. I guess once a child always a child. I know that it was a struggle dealing with us as children and it was a lot of work for you and Mom. But I do hope that as you look back on it now, you can say that it was indeed worth the effort.

I am so proud of you and what you are doing with the children at Payne Elementary School. One never really knows the difference we make in the life of a child. Helping children to learn how to read is the most important thing that they can experience. They will always appreciate the love and attention that you provide for them. When I saw this gift, I thought of the special touches that you have given to those children.

My Dad

I am proud that you are my dad
From whom all of my being exists
And with your continued faith in me
I can always do my best!

May God continue to bless you! I love you, Dad, for now and always,
Your squirrel,
Yvonne

(DECEMBER 1997)

> *NOTE: Of course, there is another story behind the nickname "Squirrel"!*

> "There's a story behind everything... But behind all your stories is always your mother's story... Because here is where yours begins." –Mitch Albom

My Best Friend

Sometimes I don't know where to begin or when I realized Ella Mae (whether May or Mae) was indeed my best friend. As I look at her now, I see the infant smoothness of her facial features and the warmth of her tender smile. But under that, I sense the tenseness and the stresses of the years of surviving and struggling. I feel the comfort and the somewhat relaxing attitude she possesses. Now those around her have grown up and seemingly developed lives of their own. Her caring spirit still exists but the strain of life preparation is no longer that pressure box, which at times seemed to have left her dumbfounded. I watched her just today so spry and light-hearted, so bouncy in nature. Yet, there is a semblance of tiredness that emits just ever so slightly in her voice and eyes like the last chords of a record being played on the old hand-cranked Victrola.

I see her now moving rapidly through the local grocery and retail stores (Basics, K-Mart, Shoppers Food) where we would be every Saturday, jockeying for position with her cart up and down each aisle enjoying the fame of "What's on sale?" "Where's the next bargain?" and "What do you think?" I see the gleam of excitement in those brown, deep-set eyes like a toddler's first Christmas as I suggest a quiet lunch at Dino's, our favorite Italian restaurant, or the Red Lobster with its seafood specialties. I feel the happiness that glows from her smile as I order for her that chilly Pina Colada as an extra added feature.

I've never known anyone who has devoted her entire life to reaching a goal as I have witnessed in my best friend. I can visualize her now hunched over that old, black Singer sewing machine until the wee hours of the morning, adding the final touches to someone's frock (as she would call it), for which she only charged a few pennies so the bills could be paid. I sensed her admiration to please everyone, sometimes neglecting herself in the process. I sensed the love she continually displayed to the children in the neighborhood, adopting them as her own, wiping the tears after a fall, and listening so attentively as they revealed their thoughts to their other "mom." I sense that closeness, which she so freely gave to others, but I know she sometimes wished she had received the same thoughtfulness from those who mean so much to her. I see within my best friend the vigor of a track star always running toward that finish line to bring joy and happiness to others.

Yet, I still sense that loneliness. The loneliness after having the thought, where did my life go? What have I accomplished? What do I have to show for it? I sense the feeling of "Did I do the right thing?" or "Could I have made better decisions?" And now, as we sit quietly talking about the childhood I so despised at times, I listen to her explain the whys of certain decisions that had to be made. I do understand. And now, as we share the challenges and successes of two adult women, I can truly feel the devotion and dedication she has always given to my being.

While she gallantly saunters through the shopping malls and curiously makes inquiries about my life; she reveals unknowingly her own feelings, which were for so long subdued like the dark caverns that contain a cadre of treasures. I listen. I share. I love!

My best friend is my mother.

(MOTHER'S DAY, MAY 1987)

Mom's Words

Mom joined God's angels on February 8, 2017. At the funeral, my siblings and I decided to offer our own personal glimpse of this special person. I decided to share a part of Mom's story written in her own words.

In 1942, Mom graduated from Manassas Industrial School and was valedictorian of her senior class. She would share her story with me of how Mr. Smith, her Latin teacher, required she not only write her speech but also memorize this eight-page handwritten oration of which I still have the original copy. This speech is 75 years old, and Mom was 18 years old at the time.

Mom begins her speech by highlighting one main question for her class: where are you going? Mom goes on to describe how the world at that time was "one in which there was a perpetual struggle." She talks about the war and the possible vocations her classmates may choose.

Mom's speech includes citations from theologians and philosophers providing insight and guidance for future success. But more importantly, Mom highlighted five key principles to overcoming struggles her classmates may face. And while these words were written by Mom 75 years ago, not only are they appropriate for today's world, but they also provide some insight into who Mom was. God was shaping Mom into who we would know her to be.

Here are some excerpts of Mom's own words:

Mom's Key Principles for Success

First is **initiative**—the power of seeing for oneself what ought to be done and going ahead doing it. You can see for yourself how important that is and how much better off the world would be if there were more persons with that go-getting, that self-assertion, a "must" prerequisite for success.

Then there is the **willingness to serve**, a second essential to overcoming. Be ready to act or help voluntarily or whenever asked to do. Don't always wait until you are forced to do something but do it willingly.

A person who lives only for himself and not to aid the betterment of his fellowmen and his race as well as himself should never have lived. Your education should not make you grow away from the common people.

A third vital element necessary is **ingenuity**, the quality of being skillful, and the power of inventing or devising. This does not mean you have to be another Edison, a

Marconi, an Alexander Graham Bell, or some other outstanding genius of science or arts.

Thousands upon thousands of humble people like you are unconsciously making just as great a contribution toward building a world as the genius of science. However, if we cannot invent, we may at least improve; we may give something of novelty to that which is old; we may reduce to simplicity that which is difficult; cleanness to that which was obscure, and vitality to that which is dead and drab.

A fourth thing that without which one can never overcome is **sticking to whatever your mind is set on in spite of difficulties**. There is no royal road to anything. Some men give up when they have almost reached their goals; while others, on the contrary, obtain a victory by exerting, at the last moments, more vigorous efforts than before. It is said by McCune that if a man has any brains at all, let him hold on to his calling and in the grand sweep of things, his time will come at last.

Of all these the one of which I am about to speak now is of greatest importance – **honor**, It is the way one looks at the things he does. It is that something in a person that makes him duty-bound to do right in all of his relations. The biblical way of putting it might be this "What if a man gains the whole world and loses his own soul?" Joseph Addison says that it is better to die a thousand deaths than wound your own character; character or honor or call it what you may is the foundation stone of all conquest.

Thus as we leave and say farewell to a school that has attempted to aid us in the answering of the question, "Where are you going?" May we say farewell with an assurance of self-confidence that we have our road maps before us and we know exactly where we are going because we have studied the signs along the way, and have made a careful check on the cost; and all set to go. Farewell.

And to those who knew Mom or more affectionately known as "Ms. Ella," let us remember she has left us a legacy to follow and has outlined her footprints for our success.

Farewell, Mom. You will be missed.

(FEBRUARY 2017)

> NOTE: Mom's Certificate of Membership in the National Honor Society of Secondary Schools of the Jennie Dean Chapter, dated November 1941, hangs proudly on the wall in my den. Mom enjoyed school and spoke once about wanting to be a teacher.

More Thoughts from My Mom (Ms. Ella)

(Excerpts from the Peace Baptist Church 100th Anniversary Questionnaire)

> To her church family: I enjoy meeting people! Learning their names and keeping in touch with them outside of church. Calling them on the

phone if they are absent from church to make sure they are fine; sending them a birthday card if I know the date. Things just to show I care. (*I used to tell Mom she had her own Pew Ministry!*)

Decide what you would like to do with your life. Then work really hard, through "thick and thin," until you reach your goal. Don't let anyone tell you that you can't do something. Show them that YOU CAN!

Let's go back to looking out for one another and helping those we can in any small way possible. For those who know me, remember me for the kind person you thought I was. For those who do not know me, I just tried to be a good person and nice to all. Love one another.

Mom's last quote: "Do What You Can, While You Can, and When You Can!"

> "A strong woman has faith that she is strong enough for the journey. But a woman of strength has faith that it is in the journey that she will become strong."
> —Luke Easter with Dee Cheeks

Emotionally and Mentally Drained but Spiritually Uplifting

2017 was an unusual year for my family. With four family deaths, it was an emotional time. My uncle passed away first (January), followed by my mom (February), my sister-in-law (October), and her mother (December). The scripture says God will provide all our needs and never give us more than we can handle—but I had my doubts. Settling estates and planning funeral services left very little time for grieving. Persons constantly asked me how I was doing, and I would respond—emotionally and mentally drained but spiritually uplifted.

I remember helping my cousin to clear out my uncle's house— the photos, letters, memorabilia, and just plain, old stuff that highlighted aspects of his journey. The accumulation of one's treasures can indeed tell a story. When my mom (Ms. Ella) passed, I felt like an "orphaned adult." I am unmarried and have no children. I suddenly became the matriarch of the family and mentally, for me, that was an unforeseen expectation. Already dealing with my own personal challenges, I felt I had no time for myself and assumed everyone would be depending on me. In the past, I had been identified as having control over everything. I was in charge. However, now, I wanted to relinquish all those responsibilities and merely enjoy what the next leg of my journey would entail. We always say life is short, but sometimes we live our lives as if we are going to be here forever. The truth is, we are not.

Yes, I am emotionally drained and feel so alone. I miss my mom, who indeed was my confidant and friend. I miss the laughter, the sharing, the ongoing support, and the togetherness we felt all those years. Mom was 93 years old when she joined God's angels, but she lived each day to the fullest. Stage one hit in 2002 when my dad passed, but I still had Mom. Those fifteen years were great! But now, I feel a sadness in my soul and as if I am just existing. I know, over time, it will get better.

God has helped me this far in my journey, and I know He will continue to do so because I believe. Part of my morning prayer thanks Him for allowing me to just touch the hem of His garment. My mom was a seamstress and, on occasions, I would hem the dresses she made for people. Sometimes, just a "touch" is needed.

We never know what paths in life our journeys may lead us, but I truly believe God uses angels to lift us up, especially in our darkest hours.

> "Are not the angels ministering spirits sent to serve?"
> (Hebrews 1:14a)

I look around for my angels on the earth who continue to keep me uplifted. I take the time to enjoy the silence so I can relive many of those memories of happiness and joy.

Life is indeed a journey with emotional waves of highs and lows. I am emotionally and mentally drained, but I thank God for keeping me spiritually uplifted.

(AUGUST 2021)

> "Sometimes you will never know the value of a moment until it becomes a memory." –Dr. Seuss

CHAPTER FIVE

FINDING MY WAY

"Everything that limits us we have to put aside." –Richard Bach

WHITNEY HOUSTON'S SONG, "I Didn't Know My Own Strength" is one of my favorites. The heartbreaks and the life busters can leave you without purpose or hope and totally rejected. But with God's help, you can pull yourself up and move forward. Sometimes, we find our way by helping others. The opportunity to serve others awakens a waning heart.

Trapped

Why must I feel so trapped?
My wings held down like
The weight of pressurized air
Invisible but restraining.

How can one be so happy
And yet so sad?
Can the freedom that one searches for
Ever be found?
Is it just not meant for everyone?
Or is it just something that must
Be continuously fought for?

Surrounded by many and
Still, I cry alone.
No one understands my need
To be set free
To flutter the realms of the earth
Like Jonathan Livingston Seagull
To explore the spaciousness of
The aqua blue sky
To stretch, to seek, to want
To experience touching the outer limits
Of my heart and soul
To leave myself and then return.

But instead, I sit and visit
As if there is no hope
No shimmer of light
No chance.

(MAY 1988)

Time

Time is an endless matter
An infinite state of being
And our existence in time
Is but a tiny millisecond
So limited...
Yet, within that small frame
Our spaces are constantly crowded
With experiences of joy and sorrow...

(JUNE 1987)

Untitled

I do not know
From whence I came
Nor do I care.

I do not know
To where I may be going
Nor is it important.

I will drift mindlessly
Across the waves of existence
Never to know why I came
Or where I will go after.

Listen… Quiet now…
They say silence is golden.
They lie.
It's lonely.

Maybe no one understands
Because I don't understand.
How can I explain it to them
When I really can't explain it to myself?

(MAY 1988)

One Easter Sunday 1987

This Easter was quite special. The ladies of "Peyton Place, Culpepper that is," Esther Jean (my aunt), Ella Mae (my mom), Grandma Julia, and I, attended church services and spent quiet time reminiscing the good old days looking at pictures.

The three generations began the day at 4:00 a.m. when the alarm, which sounded more like one of those bomb alerts, rang forever in my ears. Early sunrise service was next on the agenda. The Sperryville church was approximately 17 miles from the farm. To be there by 6:00 a.m. for the service was an experience. We traveled those narrow roads, some dirt, in the wee hours as darkness still prevailed. On arrival at two minutes past six, we found the services underway.

The small quaint Baptist church filled with an awe of spiritual relief emitted a feeling of warmth as we tip-toed through the door. I felt very proud sitting there with my aunt, grandmother, and mom. Three generations, three individuals, three survivors. Each having experienced several of life's many challenges as told by the deep seriousness in the pairs of brown eyes that, at times, signaled a glow of steadfastness. I felt special as I looked again at the threesome.

Breakfast after the service was personal. We engaged in light talk as we all consumed eggs, sausages, rolls, juice, coffee, and milk. These were special times for those who hadn't seen each other in a while. We shared the news of grief and happiness like the common bond that unites most families. A special time prevailed as the small room crowded with parishioners of all ages were beginning the day with an uplifting certainty.

Upon returning home, the old pictures were pulled from the sacred dresser drawer. A picture of my great grandmother, still very much visible, was attached to her marriage license dated July 26, 1887, from the state of Rhode Island. There were also photos of my aunt and mother in the early 1940s looking like models in some part of a *Vogue* magazine, a baby photo of my mom, then 64, had a resemblance to my niece, who was eight years old at the time. My mom's report card was amazing! Outstanding grades were indicated in all subject areas—English, social science, math, and home economics. On the graduation list, Mom successfully completed her requirements and majored in home economics, which was the only major for girls at the time. Agriculture and building construction were designed strictly for the boys.

At one point, my grandmother expressed a feeling of discontent as she had wanted to send my mother to college, but finances were unavailable. More photos of classmates and weddings brought the history of the family alive. My mother had written cute little messages on each picture. I remember one: "I'm lost" as she stood silently in the fields.

This was indeed a special Easter.

(APRIL 1987)

"Therefore encourage one another and build each other up." (1 Thessalonians 5:11a)

"If either of them falls down, one can help the other up." (Ecclesiastes 4:10a)

Saving Broken Wings

My pastor recently said to me I was always saving broken wings. I had to think about that for a moment and concurred there was some validity to the statement. Even when I was a youngster, I remember thinking I wanted to be a teacher so I could sincerely help those who could not help themselves. I wanted to work in those environments that were unfortunately labeled as impoverished, disadvantaged, and forgotten.

But there is also some resemblance to that statement, even in my personal life. I have heard comments in my inner circle that "You really saved me," or "You really helped me," or "I hear you have such a philosophical approach to your thinking." But let me be real! That comes from facing life's experiences and recovery.

What is wrong with saving broken wings? Don't we all wonder what our unique gifts are? Is it wrong to continue to reach out to those who need a helping hand? I recently saw a Facebook post that stated: "You attract damaged people when you have a healing spirit. Be careful with that. Because darkness is drawn to your light… #everybodydontwantthehealing."

I had to give some thought to that post. So true, some broken wings will remain broken, regardless of what you try to do. Even when you feel you can recognize people's gifts, they may not be ready to receive that information. The downfall is twofold—you are wasting your time and they are wasting their blessings.

A Broken Wing

I saw a broken wing today,
Fluttering in its midst
Lost in the struggle called life
With no feeling of self-worth.

I saw a broken wing today.
It was thinking that it was whole
Navigating through the daily routines
Unsure of what tomorrow brings.

I saw a broken wing today,
Stuck in life's past miseries
Unknowingly covering the sadness
That can bring one to its knees.

I saw a broken wing today
Needing an opportunity to fly.
I reach out—hold on
All is not lost.

I saw a broken wing today,
In the need of healing.
I am here where you are
No need to travel this path alone.

(NOVEMBER 2019)

ESCAPE

Imprisoned in the walls of study
The tantalizing breeze from the window
Flirts playfully with my eagerness
To get up and run!

Let me out! Let me go!
The warmth prevails for the first time
Unfolding itself from
The grips of winter.

My mind is escaping from the endless trap
That helplessly encases my body.
Stretch! Reach out!

I can close my eyes
And touch the freshness
Of the new season.

Hello, spring!

(MARCH 1988)

Untitled

I see the young sparrow
Savoring the flavors of spring
Fluttering, passing the bars of the windows
Confining me to a place within
The joy of freedom
Hurry bell!
I too want to spread my wings!

(MARCH 1988)

CHAPTER 6

Expectations and Experiences

"Every experience in your life is being orchestrated to teach you something you need to know to move forward." –Brian Tracy

"Every day starts with some expectations. But every day ends with some experience. This is Life!"
—Facebook Post by Unknown Author

We all travel this journey called life with various expectations. But what really forms us? Is it the cultural norms we grow up with? Or is it the expectations and sometimes fantasies that wave ever so gently in our hearts and minds? We are told to set goals, but whose goals are we setting—our own or our influencers'? Growing up, we were expected to follow the rules and ask no questions.

Adhering to the routines of the previous generations was the prescribed blueprint.

I think of my own upbringing—born in 1950 when children were seen but not heard. During my teenage years, the country was restless with the civil rights movement pushing for better opportunities for those who felt they were left behind. I remember the riots of 1968, the same year I graduated from high school. My parents had instilled in me the importance of a good education. Although they never had the chance to attend college, they pushed me to excel. My parents expected me to take advantage of opportunities and do better than they did. To cite an old cliché—failure was not an option.

Sometimes the pressures of expectations can lead to unforeseen experiences. Academic success in high school led me to attend Immaculata Junior College, a small, Catholic, two-year, all-girls college in the city. I was under a work scholarship program. I began my college experience being only one of four African American women in attendance. My commitment to work hard led me to not only graduate with honors but I also became vice president of the graduating class. This experience led me on the road to the University of Maryland and a chance to become a teacher.

When I became a teacher, those expectations to succeed were incorporated into my students' learning. There were some student stories of plight, abuse, and homelessness saddled with hope for the future if only someone believed in them. However, I expected all of my students to be the best. High standards with a heart of humbleness transcended. This resulted in me embracing a special bond with my students, parents, and colleagues that elevated into a high level of trust and genuine concern. These relationships continue to this day. It was important for me to know if what I did made a difference.

All expectations may not result in positive experiences. But expectations can become learning experiences. We place expectations on people we love and, at times, only find sorrow. We place expectations on our careers to only find setbacks. We place expectations on ourselves for perfection to only discover the flaws we carry. I remember when I lost my eyesight, a friend gave me a book by Willie Jolley, *A Setback is a Setup for a Comeback*. When challenges occur, we are expected to rebound. Despite my vision troubles, I was able to complete my Ph.D. program in Educational Policy at American University in 2009. The support and motivation from family, friends, and my university community were overwhelming. I realized that a bounce-back can lead to more unexpected experiences.

Life happens! I have come to believe that it is the "EE Effect" that impacts who we are. Our expectations and experiences help define our characters and beliefs, some of which can be negative or positive. So many of our exposures in life go unnoticed. We rarely take the time to reflect and uncover the meaning of what we do and why we do it. However, one thing is certain: our reactions to these elements also guide us through our journeys.

THE EE EFFECT

We live a life of expectations
Whose expectations
Yours or mine?

(SEPTEMBER 2021)

One Inch Away from Lunacy – But Thank God for that One Inch!

Life-changing experiences happen all the time. The not-so-recent 9/11 attacks forced life-changing experiences on those immediately impacted. But also, the rebound effect has continued to drastically change the lives of others forever. This story is not of such devastation. It is not about famous athletes or the rich and the famous who have always shined in the public's eyes. It is about an ordinary person and the sudden impact of a life-changing experience.

On April 11, 2003, I mingled and joked with my students that spring break was the following week and I could finally get some much-needed rest. Although at that time I had really enjoyed my 30 years in the field of education, it was always a blessing to take a break! I will never forget during the seventh period (the last class of the day) I felt as if the vision in my left eye was a bit cloudy. I knew it was time to change my contact lenses, so I attributed the brief lack of visibility to that fact. Upon arriving home, I immediately changed the lenses and prepared for the weekly Friday night sports event—bowling. It was during the second game that I once again experienced this slight problem with my vision. No pain or discomfort was associated with it, so I just assumed I was tired.

I was planning to leave that Sunday for Hilton Head, South Carolina, for an escape from the day-to-day madness that occurs in the city. The death of my father that past November was still somewhat fresh in my thoughts and getting away for a while seemed the appropriate thing to do.

And that is when the nightmare began! When I awoke that morning, Saturday, April 12, 2003, I noticed something was strange about the vision in my left eye. It was approximately 5:21 a.m. and about the time Roxie, our mixed American bulldog, would be ready for her morning walk. I realized I could not see. No, I am not talking about a little vision problem. I am saying my sight was gone! All I could see was blackness. I laid my head back on the pillow hoping I was just dreaming. I opened my eyes and, once again, blindness. At that point, I ran to the bathroom mirror to see if I could determine what was wrong. The mirror merely stared back at me without any indication there was a problem. Both eyes looked fine, but I still could not see out of the left one. I went back to the bedroom and sat in the chair. I was in total amazement. There was no pain, no physical scars, but I was blind in my left eye.

I awakened my husband at the time and said I needed to go to the emergency room because I was having a stroke. You must understand who I am. I have always worked hard. I was completing my doctoral studies at the American University and was the assistant principal at a middle school in the city. I enjoyed spending time with family and friends, attending church, reading, and bowling. I have always been extremely active and on the go. Sickness, other than an occasional cold during the winter, did not exist for me. I was too busy to be sick. I used to have a saying that "The Devil had to ride someone else's back because he had no ticket to be on mine." But this Saturday was a life-changing experience.

At the hospital, it was determined I had a detached retina. Although I have worn glasses or contacts most of my adult life and had my eyes checked on a regular basis, I had no clue what a detached retina meant. The emergency room ophthalmologist contacted a retina specialist (outside the hospital) and I was going to be seen that day. After arriving at the National Retina Institute in Chevy Chase, Maryland, I was informed my retina was completely detached, and the sooner I had surgery, the better my chances were of recovering my vision. The process of inserting a gas bubble was explained to me and I read the information package concerning a detached retina.

On Monday, April 14, 2003, I had my first surgery. This was only the beginning of a series of surgical procedures to restore my eyesight. The first surgery was not successful, so a second surgery was completed on April 23, 2003. The doctors informed me that my retina had several tears. I was asked if I remember injuring my eyes during childhood; however, at times, I could barely remember what I did the week prior (senior moments).

The six to eight-week recovery time was to begin. Most of my days were spent lying on the bed with my head hanging over the side (at least three hours straight), the required position as a part of the recovery process. The television commercials for cars were always touting their ability to go from 0 to 60 in several seconds. I felt as if my life had gone from 60 to 0 in several days. All activities ceased. No more going to school where I enjoyed working closely with my students who had given me the nickname "Mama Coates," no more driving and picking up Mom to hang out in the mall and eating at restaurants, no more bowling, no more going to the gym, and no more doctoral studies. I was 52 years old and my life had come to a standstill.

The month of May came and went. I slowly began to feel a little better and that there was hope of returning to some semblance of normalcy. Then there was Sunday, June 1st.

Sitting in my sister's basement attempting to look at some movie on their large screen television, I realized once again I could not see. The bit of vision I did have as a part of the recovery process was vanishing. Although only family members were present, I could not utter the words, "I can't see!" from my lips again. The initial toll had taken a lot, not just out of me but also my family. Another visit to the doctor's office revealed that scar tissues had formed and more surgery was required. My hopes of seeing again soon vanished. I realized I would not be returning to school to see my eighth-graders at the promotional exercise.

My left eye still presented a challenge. On August 29, 2003, another procedure was needed because, now, the eye pressure in the left eye was too low. More silicone oil was added and I had to be extremely careful of any movements. The vision in my left eye was very limited. The recovery time for a detached retina varied as with most illnesses. But I was determined to fight so that I could get my life back. There were moments I felt as if I was one inch away from lunacy. I told a friend one day I was mentally "on the bridge and I could see the water below."

Someone asked me what I learned from this experience. My reply was as follows:

> I have learned that faith can guide you through the darkest hours. Without my faith in God, I don't know if I could continue to go forward with

this life-changing experience. The power of prayer to guide you when you need it most is awesome.

My love for family and my family's devotion to me provided the support I needed. Aunt Nellie continuously reminded me that this was now the time for the family to do for me instead of me worrying about doing for others. I had to learn how to receive instead of always giving and servicing those in my circle.

And I learned the importance of service. Even in your darkest times, there is still some purpose for your life. I considered myself a "learned" woman. I was always reading and researching. I was always actively involved in helping others help themselves. But for a moment, I had forgotten all of that. No, I had not developed the "pity party" attitude, but I had difficulty determining what I was to do. I realized I could still do it but on a more limited basis. I had to adjust to the new normal.

We all experience "train derailments" in our lives. My life-changing experience may seem very simple and minor to others who have had far greater challenges. But it is not about the type of life-changing experience; it is more about the mental and physical anguish that occurs. It strengthens you to hold on. "One inch away from lunacy, but thank God for that one inch."

Note: Special thanks to Dr. Sam Mansour, my retina specialist, who continues to educate me, motivate me, and 'hold my hand' throughout this part of my journey.

(SEPTEMBER 2003)

TRUST YOURSELF

Life is filled with adventures. Why not take a leap and enjoy?
Find your passion in life. Seek what inspires your soul.
Whether it is traveling the high seas or spending time alone,
Find purpose in your life and let the journey begin.
Don't waste time; it is the one thing we can't stop.
But embrace your time as you know it and live life to the fullest.
Oh, the ups and downs may come your way,
But learning comes with evolving, so don't be dismayed.

Life is filled with adventures. Reach out and grab a few.
Reflecting is important because we rarely take the time.
Our lives of hustle and bustle consume our time to think.
Step back, reflect, and renew!
For, understanding those experiences can prepare us for this path.

Life is filled with adventures. Don't let them pass you by. Because we will wake up one morning and it will have passed us by.
Say kind words; give someone a hug.
Explore different cultures; learn to observe.
Reach out and help others along the way.
Find your passion, regardless of what others say!
Life is filled with adventure!
Take a leap and enjoy!

(CARNIVAL SUNRISE CRUISE, JULY 2019)

CHAPTER SEVEN

GROWTH THROUGH CONNECTIONS

> Katsumoto: I wish to learn.
> Nathan Algren: Read a book.
> Katsumoto: I would rather have a conversation.
> From *The Last Samurai* (2003 movie)

Are We That Different?

Well, I have just had another trip of a lifetime. Traveling has allowed me to experience the various cultures and practices that occur around the world. Whether it was walking the Great Wall of China (which was a childhood dream), strolling with the penguins on the Falkland Islands, indulging in the food and drinks of the Caribbean, or seeing the natural, peaceful surroundings in Antarctica, the exposure to our world only heightens my curiosity. While I participate as a tourist, I am always amazed at how the normal daily routines are no different from our own for everyone, no matter where they live. This last trip (a 30-day excursion from Rome to Singapore with the Princess Cruise Lines) was truly a grand adventure and my trip around the world!

From Rome to the Middle East, people are just people. It is so unfortunate we stereotype individuals without having the opportunity to experience their world. I remember when I visited Turkey several years ago, I recall the hesitancy of friends and family about the problems that existed there and why I should think twice. But don't we experience unfortunate incidents in our own country? Does that make us all bad? My motto is, "Life is to be lived and the best way to live life is to see life."

This time I visited Europe, the Middle East, and Asia, all with their own distinct characteristics, and what a learning experience it was. Transiting through the Suez Canal with Africa on one side and Asia on the other was extraordinary. Looking at the sand dunes, having lunch in a Bedouin tent in Jordan, riding one of the fastest elevators in the world's tallest building (Burj Khalifa) in Dubai, having tea at a seven-star Emirates Hotel in Abu Dhabi, and drinking a Singapore Sling on the 70th floor of the Swiss Hotel the Stanford in Singapore were adventures I will never forget. However, it is not just visiting the tourist attractions that fascinates me; it is the interactions I have in meeting and conversing with people around the world that best excite my traveling.

My thoughts and feelings at the end of these experiences were: "We are more alike than we are different. No matter where we are."

NOT MUCH DIFFERENT

The faces of the people not much different from my own
Trying to deal with life's challenges as the day goes on.
A wave of inspiration, a smile of comfort shared
A true connection to others without a word being said.

I look across the masses, a feeling of anticipation exists
As we enter the magnificent mosques filled with historical respect
We sense the dedication and love for their faith
While curiosity prevails for exploring the rest.

We tiptoe into the lives of others
Unknowing how it changes our own
To realize that we are all humans
People with devotions, love of family, and beliefs.

But while others may tend to hesitate
Because they seem unwilling to open their hearts
To learn, to listen, and to understand
Recognize the connections as we co-exist.

(APRIL 2020)

The Missing Touch

The lockdown during this 2020 COVID-19 pandemic has left us wondering if we are just "to live" or if we will be "really living." It is important to recognize that life as we know it will never be the same. Waiting for the "normalization," which is so uncertain, leaves us more concerned about the future of humanity. Did we lose something along the way? Did we lose focus on what was more important? Whatever philosophical theory one chooses to embrace, the results are the same—we have been changed!

Discussions abound on the human and economic suffering that this generation of people must adhere to with unforeseen adjustments. We are confined to our personal spaces with limited opportunities to feel anxiety-free when we leave the doors of our homes. Our routines and rituals have been stripped from the souls of our society, leaving us in a cloud of uncertainty and stress. What do we do? Where do we go from here? What direction should we choose?

However, it is the inability to touch that impacts us most. Having watched several virtual funerals, my heart aches to realize our need to embrace our loved ones is now taboo. Love was affectionally displayed through "a touch." We can no longer gather with our friends. Travel is suspended. Connections are now virtual. But what happens to "the touch"? I remember the lyrics of an old Diana Ross song: *Reach Out and Touch (Somebody's Hand)*.

Our connections with others propel us to move forward. Our relationships, not our routines, develop us, inspire us, and expand our horizons. And while we are existing in a more technologically-driven society, the question becomes can we now survive without that human touch?

I Saw the Face

I saw the face on the screen
Worn and torn and somewhere in between.
The eyes drawn dark with such despair
And no one around to show some care.

I saw the face on the screen
Lost to the world
Feeling overwhelmed by the new life
Alone in thought and saved by prayer.

I saw the face on the screen
Drained of hope but not of faith
Wondering what is to come
For the day seems too long.

I saw the face on the screen
Longing to touch, to hug, to scream
I am here; do you not see me?
Lost without that touch.

I saw the face on the screen
Waiting for the day
When all is well with the world
The warmth, the security, the calmness.

I saw the face on the screen.
It is mine.

(JULY 2020)

Feeling One's Soul

The connections we make change us forever.
Experience and exposure enhance our capabilities.
The inner beauty of it all—so uplifting, so serene
We enjoy the calmness as we sit idly by
As the waves of the ocean offer us tranquility.
Calmness!
How often do we experience this pleasure?
Deep in our souls, loving, and caring
Where that peace unfolds.
It's like feeling the wind—guiding us to parts unknown.
Rage, go away! There is no place for you.
For the rays of the sun radiate and heal.

Stand still and listen as our hearts cry out.
Peace is around the bend if we only allow its entrance.
Wait—I hear that voice in my ear.

Whispers of calmness, love, and sharing
Is it not our souls that make us who we are?
Drifting, drifting, until we feel nothing at all.

(JULY 2019)

CHAPTER EIGHT

CHANGE IS INEVITABLE

"Do not conform to the pattern of this world, but be transformed by the renewing of your mind." (Romans 12:2a)

"You can't have a physical transformation until you have a spiritual transformation." –Cory Booker

IN OUR LIFETIME, THE one thing that is the most difficult to face is change. Change forces us to rethink how we have lived our lives and, more importantly, how we will prepare for the future. It does not matter if it is a physical, emotional, or spiritual journey. In the end, you can emerge like a butterfly spreading your wings for the flight ahead.

As we continue our journey in life, we are constantly being transformed. One of my favorite holiday films is Dr. Seuss' animated version, "How the Grinch Stole Christmas." I spoke so much about the antics of the Grinch in that story that one year, my students presented me with the VHS tape, which I still own. (Well, we know how long ago that must have been!) Recently, I started thinking about what was so magical about that story that captivated my interest into adulthood. I know the music was charming and the characters in Whoville were very humble and supportive of one another. But it had to be more! What was the "nick" that kept drawing me back every year to see this show?

Now, I realize it was seeing how someone could transform from feeling totally isolated from family and friends to understanding the importance of togetherness. It is our past experiences and exposure or lack of that transform our thinking and reactions to life's circumstances. Haven't all of us at one time resented the happiness we see others portray, and wondered, why not me? While we may not swoop down into Whoville and steal all the holiday preparations, we do inadvertently say or do things we wish to make others unhappy. But what we learned from the story was that those material things did not deter the happiness and love felt by the residents of the town. Seeing this, the Grinch was transformed and, as the narrator said, "His heart grew and grew, three sizes that day."

We need to recognize trying to destroy someone else's joy only destroys our own. We all have purpose, gifts, and destinies. It really does take a village to raise not only a child but our community. Think about your own transformation as you have evolved. What was your story five years or 10 years ago? Have you transformed for the better or the worse? In the movie, "The Bucket List," Morgan Freeman asked the questions: "Have you found joy in your life?" "Has your life brought joy to others?" Freeman stated these two questions were asked by the gods at the entrance to heaven. Sometimes in life, we need to reach back and take a peep into the past so we can appreciate the now and determine which road to take as we go forward.

In life, we will continue to transform. Each day brings new possibilities, new experiences, new choices, and new reactions. Embrace your transformation, looking for the goodness that surrounds you. As a part of your destiny, reach out and offer positive solutions forgoing negativity. There is room for all of us to become better people. Instead of criticizing and chastising others without understanding their journeys, show compassion and empathy. And then maybe—your heart too can grow three sizes.

Transformed

I am not who I used to be.
For truly I have grown.
While the steps through life
Are sometimes challenging,
Lessons are learned
And I am transformed!

(JANUARY 2021)

Fall Risk

We live in a time when we are all capable of falling. Falling is not the same as failing. Sometimes these setbacks occur because of our own decisions; at times, they just happen. This is life!

After my last eye surgery, I wore two hospital bands—one said, "gas bubble"; the other said, "fall risk." With limited peripheral vision, I found myself constantly falling, especially on the stairs. When you undergo a life-changing experience, you have a choice to become stagnant or decide to move "full steam ahead." Better said than applied. It is amazing how each stage of one's journey can present its own set of desires, hopes, experiences, sacrifices, and disappointments.

There is no life reference guide providing a blueprint for us to follow. We follow our own "yellow brick road" based upon impulsive decisions, predetermined goals, and available resources. We listen or sometimes ignore the advice of others because of its relevance at that given time and space.

In today's technology, world information attacks from multiple sources. Social media rarely provides us the time to synthesize information before we react. We are glued to the immediacy, and the future of life is only a click away. We are guilty of this rapid transformation. The perception is that we text and not talk; we click and not chat. The old, limited telephone party line of yesterday is now replaced with hundreds of people having the ability to communicate simultaneously. Could this set us up for a fall risk?

Our lives are symbolic of the ebbs and flows of the ocean. At times, life feels like the blowing winds circling the sand dunes. We are continuously in a "work zone." Permanent and temporary run parallel like a two-way highway: back and forth—ahead and reverse. What can we do?

Regardless of the path we choose, at some point, we will experience a "fall risk." Do you remember the commercial slogan, "I've fallen, and I can't get up"? Life-changing experiences can indeed cause us to fall mentally, spiritually, and emotionally. However, obstacles can become opportunities, so we rise.

(OCTOBER 2021)

"Stop worrying about the potholes in the road and enjoy the journey." –Babs Hoffman

"The secret of life is to fall seven times and to get up eight times." –Paulo Coelho

CHAPTER NINE

THE JOURNEY CONTINUES

"A journey of a thousand miles begins with a single step."
—Lao Tzu

"Two roads diverged in a wood, and I—I took the one less traveled by, And that has made all the difference." –Robert Frost

A Journey Through Discovery

A journey through discovery takes endurance and patience. It doesn't matter if it is a physical, emotional, or spiritual journey. In the end, you can emerge like a beautiful butterfly spreading your wings for the flight ahead. A journey, in retrospect, allows you to discover yourself. It is the living of life, including the roadblocks you face. Mark Twain said, "The two most important days in your life are the day you were born and the day you find out why." Sometimes, we can't figure out the why because we are too focused on the who or what.

Now, at the graceful age of 70, life's journey brings a whole different perspective. The lessons learned and the experiences lived have broadened my attitude to embrace the people who come into my life and the unexpected challenges waiting around every curve. Separations through divorce, death, or displeasure can also be teachable moments. Developing positive relationships and connections built on love, honesty, and respect gives me joy and happiness. Learning about various histories and cultures has made me realize our time on the earth is indeed only a brief snippet of the cosmos. I have learned the importance of enjoying the moment in which I live. Life is too short for anything else!

When I decided to retire in 2005, one of my students asked me to write an essay on why I was leaving. While this was not the first writing assignment given to me by my students, it was the last. This is an excerpt of that essay:

> In our lifetimes, the one thing that is most difficult for us to face is change. Change forces us to rethink how we have lived our lives and, more importantly, how we will prepare for the future. What's exciting about life is that every morning offers a brand-new day with unlimited possibilities. Yesterday is gone and tomorrow

has yet to arrive. I have learned to be happy for today because thinking about tomorrow brings uncertainty. No, I have no idea what lies ahead for me, but I welcome the challenge.

The world is filled with goodness. The ebb and flow of the ocean waters remind us that nothing remains still. I find myself in search of peace and quiet. The need to rush around has been removed from my psyche. I look for calmness and pray for a long life. Life is about transitions. How we manage these transitions shapes us into who we become. We recognize the steppingstones laid before us serve only as a blueprint. We make the decision; we choose which road we take. So, we journey on!

THE JOURNEY CONTINUES

You may not know where you are going,
For the pains of yesterday
Sometimes haunt our very existence.

You may not know where you are going,
For the present is filled with pressure and impatience,
Impacting the ability to see the light ahead.

You may not know where you are going,
For the future seems too far to care
But the past and the present do prepare you for there.

You may not know where you are going,
For our futures lie in an area of unknown.
Remember the journey is not one of solitude.

You may not know where you are going.
This journey is taken by us all.
Choices are endless and dreams deterred.

You may not know where you are going.
You only know where you have been.
Open your heart; open your mind.
Peace and love!

The journey continues.

(NOVEMBER 2020)

> "The heart of a man plans his way, but the LORD establishes his steps." (Proverbs 16:9 ESV)

BIBLIOGRAPHY

Albom, Mitch. *For One More Day*. New York: Hachette Books, 2014.

Angelou, Maya. Posted on Facebook, July 5, 2011. https://www.facebook.com/MayaAngelou/posts/10150251846629796.

Bach, Richard. *Jonathan Livingston Seagull: A Story*. Tel Aviv: Boostan Mod Enterprises, 1973.

Paul Baloche. *Open the Eyes of My Heart*. CD. *First Love - Live*. Caldwell Auditorium, TX: Integrity Music, 1998.

Booker, Cory. "Cory Booker Quotes." BrainyQuote. Xplore. Accessed March 15, 2022. https://www.brainyquote.com/authors/cory-booker-quotes.

Coelho, Paulo. *The Alchemist*. New York: HarperCollins, 1993.

Duhamel, Georges. *The Heart's Domain*. New York: The Century Company, 1919.

Easter, Luke. *Gracious Spiritual Uplifts from Poetry & Rhyme Lyrics –* Poem: "A Strong Woman vs. A Woman of Strength" [Abridged version with Dee Cheeks]. Cleveland, OH: PublishAmerica, 2007.

Freire, Paulo. *Pedagogy of the Oppressed*. New York: Bloomsbury Academic, 2020.

Frost, Robert. *The Road Not Taken and Other Poems*. Boston: Digireads.com Publishing, 2017.

Giovanni, Nikki. *The Collected Poetry of Nikki Giovanni: 1968-1998*. New York: Harper Perennial, 2007.

Hoffman, Babs. "Babs Hoffman Quotes." 101shrequotes.com. Accessed March 15, 2022. http://101sharequotes.com/authors/Babs_Hoffman.

Rilke, Rainer Maria. *A Rilke Trilogy*. Boston: Shambala, 1992.

Schlatter, John Wayne. *I Am a Teacher*. Piscataway, NJ: Our Town Press, 2004.

Seuss, Dr. *Seuss-Isms!: A Guide to Life for Those Just Starting Out ... and Those Already on Their Way*. New York: Random House, 2018.

The Last Samurai. Burbank, CA: Warner Bros. Pictures, 2003.

Tracy, Brian. *Goals: How to Get Everything You Want Faster than You Ever Thought Possible*. San Francisco: Berrett-Koehler Publishers, 2010.

Tzu, Lao, and Charles Johnston. *The Tao Te Ching: Lao Tzu's Book of the Way and of Righteousness*. Kshetra Books, 2016.

Winfrey, Oprah. "Oprah Talks to Graduates about Feelings, Failure and Finding Happiness." Stanford University, June 15, 2008. https://news.stanford.edu/news/2008/june18/como-061808.html.

About the Author

Dr. Yvonne D. Coates was born and raised in Washington, D.C. In the 6th grade at Bryan Elementary School, she decided she wanted to do two things in life: become a teacher and travel to all the places in her geography book. Dr. Coates has over 45 years in the field of education. She has spent most of her professional life with the District of Columbia Public School (DCPS) as a teacher, assistant principal, workshop presenter, Assistant Director, PAUSE (an alternative school program); Assistant Director, Instructional Recruitment and Orientation Branch; and Director, Educational Credentialing and Standards Branch.

After her retirement from the school system, Dr. Coates has continued to work in the educational arena. She served for three years as the D.C. State Coordinator with the Regional Educational Laboratory (REL) Mid-Atlantic, connecting educational stakeholders with research and technical support. She was also employed as an instructor with the Paxen Learning Corporation (About Face!) where she taught in an after-school program focusing on life skills for middle and high school students. She is currently a University Faculty Supervisor at American University, providing instructional and classroom management support for teacher candidates.

Dr. Coates received a Ph.D. in Educational Policy from American University, an M.A in Education and Human Development (Educational Supervision) from George Washington University, a B.A. in English Education from the University of Maryland, and an A.A. in Liberal Arts from Immaculata Junior College.

While her first passion lies in education and serving others, her second one involves traveling. In her youthful years, Dr. Coates had the opportunity to backpack/camp from Washington, D.C. to the Florida Keys and to journey solo across the country on a Greyhound bus. Now, cruising has become her favorite mode of discovering those places in that 6th grade geography book. With over 30 cruises, she has traveled to Asia, Europe, South America, the Falkland Islands, the Panama Canal, Antarctica, Mexico, and the Caribbean. In 2019, her excursion aboard the Princess Sapphire was a 30-day grand adventure from Rome to Singapore transiting the Suez Canal.

Community outreach is important to Dr. Coates. She serves as Vice Chair, Board of Trustees and Chair of the Scholarship Committee at Peace Baptist Church in Washington, D.C. She remains connected with several former students, providing support as they continue to adjust to the demands of adulthood.

Dr. Coates' hobbies include teaching, traveling, bowling, writing, reading, and spending time with family and friends. Fitness is also important as she participates in POTM (Peace on the Move) classes with her church and walking in 5k events (chasing medals). This memoir is a collection of reflections and experiences as a part of her journey.

Connect with the Author

 Yvonne.Coates.90

 ydiggs212@gmail.com

www.ingramcontent.com/pod-product-compliance
Lightning Source LLC
Chambersburg PA
CBHW070255100426
42743CB00011B/2247